WITHIN ME

Kaitlyn Rightmyer

WITHIN ME

Kaitlyn Rightmyer

Book Design by Emily Lalonde: www.emilydelalonde.com.
Illustrations by George Bothamley.
Editing by Logan Miehl: www.loganmiehl.com.

Within Me by Kaitlyn Rightmyer – 1st edition

This book is based on true events. It reflects the author's present recollections of experiences over time, told with the genuine desire to invite connection and healing.

ISBN: 979-8-218-57258-7 | E-Book: 979-8-218-57259-4

The words of my journey.

The words that held me long before they were written.

For anyone trying to remember their way, may they hold you too.

CONTENTS

INTRODUCTION   1

PART ONE: BREAKING   5

PART TWO: BECOMING   47

INTRODUCTION

Within our depths lives all that we seek but have yet to maybe touch—the freedom to live intimately, truthfully, and fully alive. These words live to light the way there.

This is the story of my journey back home to myself, and much of what I have learned along the way.

What is the point of it all?

May it be to live life on the verge of tears. To wholeheartedly touch life and be touched just the same. One hand extended toward the heart of another, with the other hand always on our own. Living from this place. Allowing ourselves to be moved by love for ourselves and each other.

May you feel held by the words of this book and rediscover your own song that sings this tune of aliveness.

May you trust the journey there, and carry these words with you as you walk.

May you discover what lives between and beneath these pages.

May they shelter you and give you the sanctuary you seek.

May they wrap you in the most tender hug and remind you that you are not alone.

This world is so big, and yet so very small, as we are all meant to be holding hands in ways that join us all around it.

From within my depths and with all my love, I share these words with you—my story of breaking and becoming.

May it awaken in you the courage to give voice to your story, and keep living it in deeper and more loving ways.

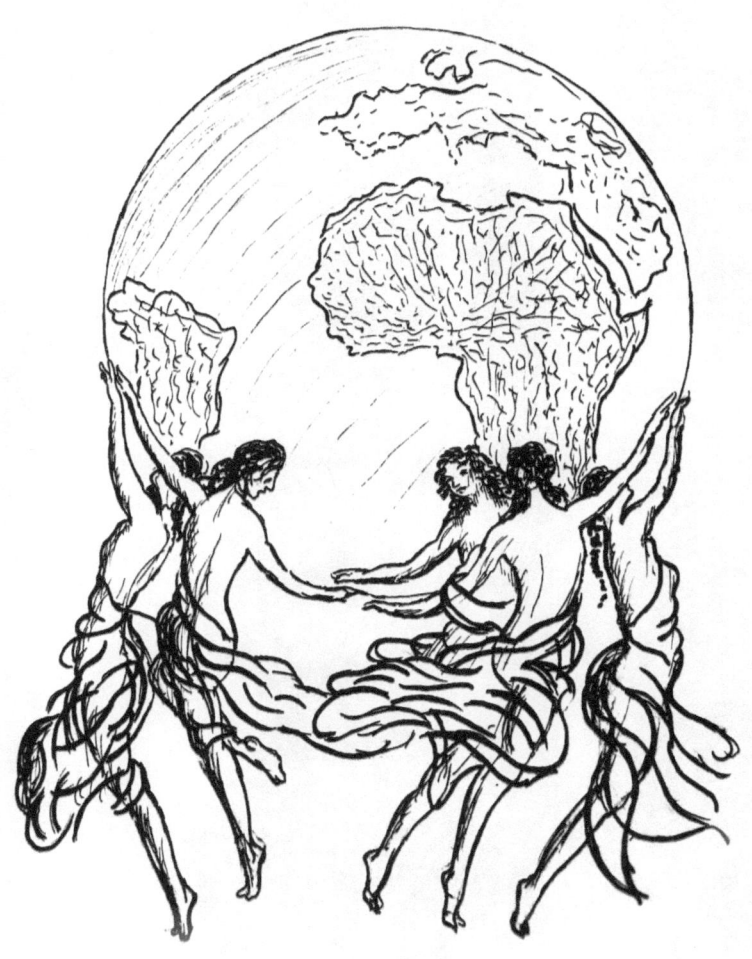

PART ONE:
BREAKING

I learned intimately, viscerally, and experientially that there are two kinds of breaking: breaking down, and breaking open. I learned that this world will stop at nothing to break me down. But through that, I also learned that life will stop at nothing to break me open and set me free.

I lived the first three decades
of my life grasping at
strings, desperately trying to
understand this world and to
recognize my place within it.

There existed a subtle sense
that no matter how hard I tried,
I never would. I spent a long
time feeling trampled by this
confusion; a life of attempting
to fit into a place I knew within
my depths I was not meant to
fit into. But if I wasn't meant to
fit into this world, where did I
belong?

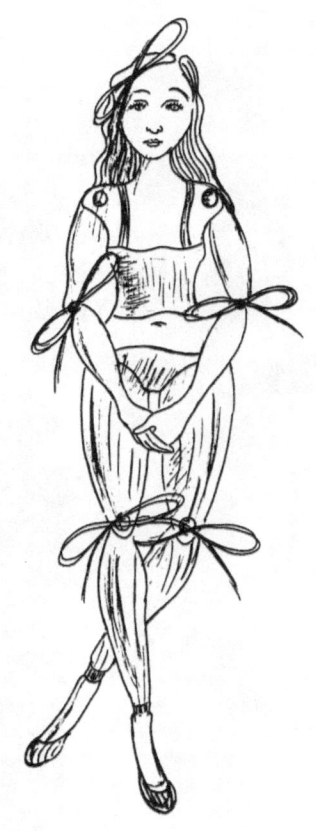

When we are breaking—both in subtle
and not so subtle ways—and we cannot
comprehend why, those true places that
dwell within us feel so very far away.
A beacon we slowly lose all sense of.
Our true north, gone to the world.

As early as when I was a young child, this
disorientation would keep me up at night.
I remember so many nights spent lying awake, eyes
wide, heart racing, gripped in terror. I always looked
at the big picture. This one was too big for my vast
heart and my tiny sense of understanding.

I felt so small in this world. Unsafe. Maybe I
would never find my way. Maybe life was like one
endless maze, with high walls that slowly inched
inward in a way that diminished my sight of the
sky. I somehow knew the sky. The view above felt
familiar to me like I knew it could show me the way,
but those metaphorical high walls...

My days were always busy when I was a
child. Mornings spent at school, evenings
spent at the dance studio or on the
soccer field. Always attempting to fit
in. I needed to be perfect at everything.
Running from one thing to the next.
The world around me was in constant
motion, and I had no time to process it.
I would not have known how to if I did.

And so, in time, all of this world—that
constantly rushed through me and in
no way made sense to me—began to live
within me. All of what was mine and all
of what was others'. I did not know the
difference. The experiences left unsorted
began to weigh down upon what I already
held that came before me. Until one
day, the nights spent gripped in terror
became days gripped in the same.

I lived most of my early life in fear. The entirety of the world scared me in an all encompassing, coming-from-everywhere, kind of way. Irrational, really. Because how could I be deeply afraid of so many things when my life had just begun?

I did not know then that what I was most afraid of was myself. Afraid of surviving in this nonsensical world with my heart in one piece. This fear bled into anything and everything. Panic became my constant companion. Eventually, there were days I could barely leave the house. They were spent in a dreadful hole. At night I paced the floor of my bedroom, afraid to be in the dark. Many tangible memories are lost from my childhood, but the recollection of these teenage years vividly remains.

I learned very early on that our vulnerability can
be used against us; our pure sensitivity turned into
something fragile. I felt so very fragile then.
I had too many cracks.

As we grow older within the walls of our wounded
sensitivity, we begin to believe any small thing
can shatter us. It becomes tremendously unsafe
to be who we are. To wear our hearts on our sleeve
for the world to see. It becomes tremendously
uncomfortable to feel deeply when all we ever feel is
a fear and a despair that we cannot seem to explain.

What was born to be our innate strength becomes a weakness we do not know how to hold. One that is used. One that is abused.

In this world, fear scares us into submission.

In this world, self-abandonment becomes a plague.

In this world, our gifts become weapons used against us.

In this world, we often become someone else entirely just to survive.

I became someone else. I became who
I thought I needed to be. I manipulated
myself in order to meet my needs because
I did not know another way to have them
met. In an unsteady environment, we
learn that doing so is the only way.

I did not know how to be in the
softness of myself. A softness
that was always violated and
was never revered. A softness
that never felt safe—that took
on everything in an attempt
to feel loved.

My edges sharpened, meeting
in jagged places. My heart
hardened like the world's.
It was a place I could not be.
Who I innately was morphed
into someone else entirely.
Like an erosion, I was slowly
chipping away over time.

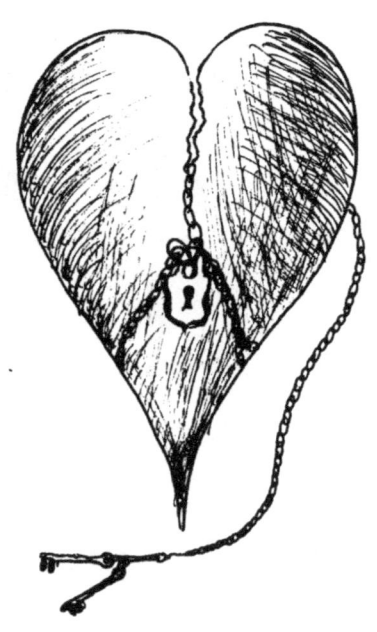

At first I did not notice the subtle ways in
which my landscape had changed.
I had been slowly sacrificing pieces of
myself in ways I didn't think would
matter. Then there were the times that
those pieces were not given,
but taken from me.

I did not know then that this erosion
would matter *in every way*. I did not
understand that each time I sacrificed
myself, my resentment intensified.
I began to begrudge the whole of the
world and everything in it.

There will come a time when we finally
gaze into the mirror and we do not
recognize who we see. There will come a
time when we do not entirely remember
who we were before the world turned us
into someone else.

"I do not know who I am," I said.

"I will tell you who to be," said the world.

In fleeting moments, we may hear the
song our soul is whispering. We mostly
cannot harmonize with it. And we
mostly ignore it. It hurts to hear. It hurts
to know how we have fallen. It hurts to
know we have been forgotten. It hurts
even more to know we have
forgotten ourselves.

At the shy age of fourteen, I signed with a
well-known modeling agency in New York City.
I grew up in this industry—a sensitive soul in
a superficial world. A mere child changing and
maturing in a tangle of scrutiny and success.
I was simultaneously glorified and rejected.

My hair was cut and my eyebrows were
bleached and my waist was shrinking. I was
booking big jobs and landing on magazine
covers. It was written that I would be the next
Claudia Schiffer, and I was dying inside.
My body was withering and so was my spirit.
I was fading away.

My tender heart only wanted to be loved.
I was killing myself for it, and yet I still
only seemed to learn that love was fickle.
I only realized years down the road that
it is not love that is fickle, but the absence
of it that is a volatile thing.

The absence of love left me with wounds and scars
and holes that felt like endless pits. They enveloped
me in a darkness that felt like it would swallow
me. I could not take back what time had done.
What would I even do if I could? I learned to cope in
whatever ways I could.

Sometimes the ways we learn to cope
fill us with shame, and that shame
causes us to shrivel.

Sometimes the ways we learn to cope
allow us to finally feel accepted.

Sometimes that acceptance feels like punishment.

The grief that came from being accepted
by the world—for being someone I was
not—gnawed at me from the inside out.
An ache in my heart. Pressure on my
lungs. A heaviness in my steps. At that
time, it was a grief I could not name.
It lived without a name for many years.

I lived hunched over in protection of
myself. A stifled and battered heart.
Did you know we do this? Did you know
we bow our posture, curling inward,
like we are wrapping our bodies around
our hearts to shield them from the
world? That, when it all becomes too
much to bear, all we know how to do
is hide as best we can? We protect our
hearts. This grief feels endless only
because there is something equally as
endless but tremendously more powerful
underneath it. We long for it.

The pain we have wears different masks. This pain, that does not have a name, lives within us, wanting to be freed. It wears masks of resentment. Masks of jealousy. Masks of anger. These masks form an impenetrable armor. We wear them to let the pain become anything other than the immense hurt we feel for simply wanting to be loved. For simply wanting to be loved but perhaps not knowing what that truly is. Or how to give it. Or how to receive it.

This pain wants to be seen, it wants to be felt, it wants to be freed, and yet we bury it so deep. We shove it down, or we give it to others because we do not know how to experience it ourselves. We do not know how to make sense of it, or feel it, or see why it is even there in the first place.

We do not know how to love what desperately wants to be heard. We do not know how because we have never been shown.

True love is a mirror. One that we have
never gazed upon before.

We are led to believe that love only ever
lets us down. Even so, we desperately try
to find that love, no matter the cost.

The cost, however, inevitably leads
to more pain when we search
in all the wrong places.

We throw our pain like daggers, at
ourselves and at others. We throw them
with the words we speak, the stories we
tell, the boxes we put people in, the hurt
we cause, and the judgments we cast.
We cannot see the pain we cause others
because we too are living in that
very same pain.

Believe me when I tell you that beneath
my pain lived a longing—a thread woven
through my life, reminding me that
something was missing. My longing for
more was something I could sense but
could never grasp in a tangible way.

I never seemed content with what I had.
On the surface, I appeared fickle, but deep
down, I now know it was a desperate
attempt to find that source of longing.
To grasp it with my fingers. To wrap it
around me like a blanket. To name
the nameless.

I suppose it was not so much a missing piece, but the thing that holds all the pieces together. The answer to the question I had been asking since I was born. Where did I belong? Beyond that, what kept me from feeling that, no matter where I was, I already did?

When I was 25, I married a man who
made me feel alive. For a while, it dulled
that longing for what was missing. For
a while, it felt like I was living a whole
life. *An illusion*. Because for that life to
continue to feel whole, I needed to keep
giving up more and more of myself.

To keep the peace, the edges of myself
blurred even more. In a desperate
attempt to avoid confrontation, I took
the fight within. I swallowed my words. I
fought every battle inside and eventually
never seemed to leave the trenches.
There were multiple wars, and one of
them was me against myself.
I could never be reached.

Remember when I said we throw
our pain at others like daggers?

Abuse comes in many forms, and it
comes in many ways. It is not always
conscious. This does not lessen the blow.
Within abusive circumstances, we may
be led to believe that we deserve this
abuse or are in some way responsible for
the daggers being thrown our way. There
is so much confusion that arises from
this place. What is real? What is not?

This level of devaluation inevitably leads to losing belief in our worthiness. Losing belief in our worthiness inevitably leads to losing our autonomy.

Autonomy is the ability we have to choose what is truly best for our wellbeing. What happens when we lose this ability?

What happens when our state of being becomes so entangled with another's?

What happens when we do not feel strong enough to choose?

What happens when the choices we need to make are treated as defiance?

How do we speak of the battles we are fighting within when our lives look peaceful to those who are watching?

We do not speak of them, and we are left with a crippling sense of aloneness.

There is a part of us that does not wish to speak
about such things because it would shatter the
illusion—the illusion that everything is perfect.
Because did we not need to be perfect? Who would
we be if we simply stopped upholding the façade?
Perhaps more frighteningly,
what would others think?

It takes incredible bravery to even contemplate
these questions. And yet, they become questions
our heart feels forced into asking when bravery
is the last thing we feel.

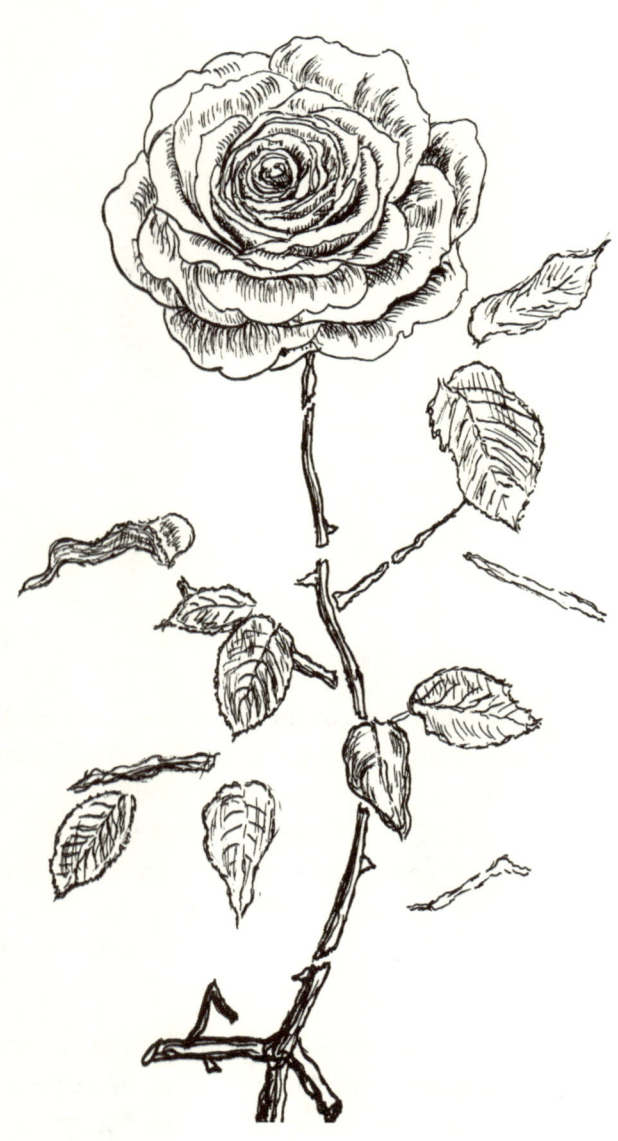

The time will come when the house of
cards inevitably falls and we will not
know where to go. We only know that we
cannot go on as we are. We plant our feet;
we suddenly refuse to take one more step
in the direction we are heading. We know
that if we do, we will destroy ourselves,
and we may destroy others, too.

A moment of reckoning. A declaration.

This world has taken away our ability to stand tall and choose from a place we know to be true. We have been choosing from shadowed places, and when we do, we do not see that our wounds are what rule us. When our wounds choose for us, that is not a choice. That is a reaction. That feels like a forced hand. An endless loop of living the same stories that we are blind to, stumbling around in the dark.

The only step now is to choose to wholeheartedly grasp what was taken. To reclaim what was lost. To make choices from places that shine. Perhaps this will be the most difficult choice of our lives because we must make it in the dark when we cannot feel the light.

The power of this choice is something that I learned in the darkest moments of my life.

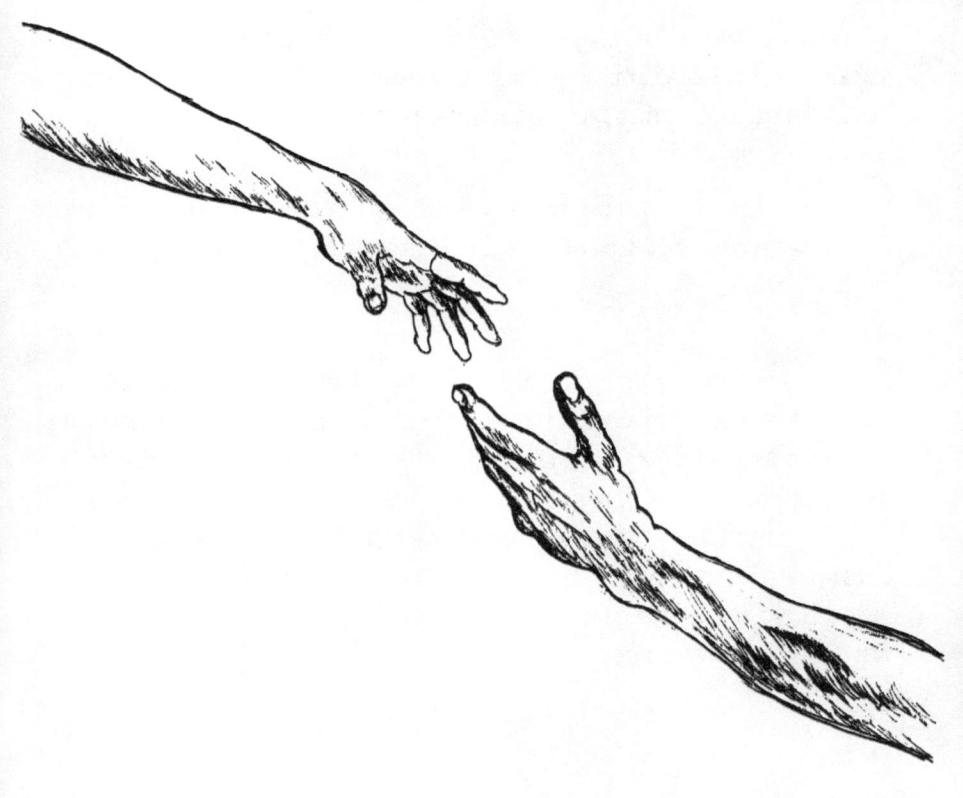

When we feel like all is lost, when we feel like we may be swallowed whole by this darkness, these are the moments that hold the choices that may change everything.

My heart knows this because my life showed this to me in more ways than one. My life showed me that what I sought was also seeking me.

Life is standing with an outstretched hand. We must reach out to meet it. She waits to meet us, but she also waits on our choice to meet her. To claim the life we deserve. We claim it in our promise to remember that we are worthy of this life. We claim it in our promise to show up for ourselves with the fullness of our hearts. Maybe we cannot make this promise right now. If so, we can vow to never stop until it is a promise we can speak with conviction.

When I turned thirty, the house of cards
I had built crumbled. I was left with what
felt like nothing but this monumental
promise. It turns out this promise
was everything.

During that time, I did not know I was
on a precipice—that this promise would
ignite the beginning of my true path.
A journey that had me meeting myself,
facing myself, and freeing myself.
All that was held within me, casting
its shadows—the fears, the façades, the
expectations, the layers of excruciating
pain. All that was holding me captive.
A journey that had me living the
questions I had carried for so long.
A journey home. A journey
within my depths.

Because, underneath and much deeper
than what we want to run from,
is who we truly are.

WITHIN ME

This promise to ourselves is everything because
it will be the only thing that holds us when we
want to give up.

In the moments we are scared beyond reason.

In the moments we feel hope is lost.

In the moments it hurts beyond what we think
we can withstand.

During the times when we fall to our knees, we
are reminded that we can rise over and over
again. We know there is always a hand to help
us up.

When I first began this journey, I did not yet know
that what I would face within would also break me.
It would break me many times and in many ways. I
did not yet know that in this breaking, I would gain
a piece of my lost self each and every time.

This world broke me down, but I chose life. I chose
to live with all of me and with more of me each time
I seemed to fall apart.

I began to give myself to the breaking,
knowing deep down that what was true
could never shatter. I was breaking open
to the real me. I witnessed it—*gosh, did
I witness it.* A different sort of breaking.
I witnessed over and over again that
maybe, just maybe, this breaking
was setting me free.

Within the depths of all of it, I began to
meet myself. Yes, this breaking hurt. It
was agonizing at times. But it was also
different. This breaking was showing me
the truth, and the truth held me. I was
becoming the answer to the question
I had been asking my whole life.

So make this monumental promise. Make this promise to life and to yourself.

Whisper it fiercely every day.

Breathe it into your bones.

Solidify it in every step you take, even when they feel backward.

Sing it into the wind and the water.

Get to know it profoundly, with the conviction of your beautiful heart.

And when all you have are your tears, let them fall and let them declare it for you.

This promise will not let you down. It cannot. It simply cannot. It does not know how to, nor would it ever wish to.

You will see how life has made this
promise for you, too, and she will hold
you as you live it. She will stand by you
as you face the aftermath of what this
world brought upon you. As you choose
your own heart. As you remember what
it means to love and truly live—your
journey of breaking and becoming.

PART TWO:
BECOMING

When we feel we are breaking, being stripped bare, we discover the presence of what can never be lost or taken away. It can never truly break. It can only blossom. What follows is the journey to become it.

The call that guides us home.

This call begins as a whisper—this
distant song beckoning us towards the
light. We cannot help but orient ourselves
to it, like how we cannot help but face the
sun wherever it shines in the sky.

We hear this call from deep within
us; a song. We hear it from all around
us because this song lives. It is woven
through all of life.

This world has attempted to mute this
song, but it remains eternally singing. It,
too, still sings deep within you.

It is time to slow down. In this world
of constant and erratic motion—in this
world of avoidance, running, competing,
and racing—it is time to slow down
and listen.

Have you ever stopped to listen to the
wind? Have you ever stopped to listen
to things you did not realize could even
make a sound? How beautiful to discover
what those things are and the music
that they make.

Perhaps we have come to a place where
we do not wish to discover such things.
Because how could there be such
beautiful things and such beautiful songs
in a world that has nearly destroyed us?
How could beauty possibly exist in a
world filled with such suffering?

We cannot accept it—that it could all
exist, all at once. We cannot accept it,
and yet there is evidence of the fact,
in this very moment, that it can. And
the only thing we must do, in this very
moment, is to gaze into the mirror or
into the eyes of another.

To *see*. We look only with
our eyes, but we *see* with our
whole bodies, with all of our
senses.

Perhaps to learn to see we
must only close our eyes
and *feel*.

We forget that, even under the darkest
of days, we are still standing amidst
what shines. We have lost touch with
this sense—our innocence. We can look at
the light, but are we really able to *feel* the
light? Can we sense that we are of it?

We are not what this world has turned
us into. We are the innocence we have
survived to protect. We are the song that
still sings and will never stop.

How do we come back to our sensitivity
that became such a fragile thing?

How do we come back to our
vulnerability that became a weapon
used to hurt us?

How do we reclaim what caused us to
stop feeling alive in the first place?

This is where we must be brave.

Our vulnerability caused our hearts
to close. We locked them up and all but
threw away the key. It became easier
to feel nothing at all. And yet, it is only
through our vulnerability that our
hearts will open once again.

We heal from the outside-in to
live from the inside-out.

We heal to be able to come back
to our hearts, where a world
untouched by this one lives.

We take back our innocence.

We relearn the ability to live
with our sensitivity—to feel
deeply and stand strongly.
Our sensitivity can hold the
strength of all that is true.
A strength that is unwavering
in its ability to stand, its
ability to face, its ability to
feel, and its ability to protect.
A strength that is found,
felt, and fortified within.
A strength that can move
mountains in the most
gentle ways.
A softness.

We are faced with finding this bravery
when all our defenses begin to crumble.
And when all our defenses begin to
crumble, we begin to hear the call. The
song that guides us home.

We feel utterly beaten down. We cannot run anymore. If we are honest, we do not really want to. We are beginning to be stripped bare of pretense, but we do not know how to allow it. It possibly feels like the end. What may feel like the end turns into the most profound beginning.

Endings feel like we are dying, and indeed, in many ways, we are. We will die many times over on this journey of becoming. But dying is not the end. It is a means to being revived and reclaimed. A transformation. Let this true meaning of endings seep into your skin like the warmth of the sun. Because that is what they are. They are beginnings.

I remember this beginning. I remember
how for so long it felt like
I had been dying.

I remember the moment the front
door closed after he left. It happened so
quickly, and yet maybe not so quickly at
all. Because if I truly acknowledge it, it
had been a long time coming. Long before
where I then found myself. Years of
avoidance and pretending. That was how
it came to implode. Even though it had
been a long time coming, I felt so utterly
unprepared for that moment when I
stood alone at that front door.

I had felt alone for such a long time,
really, but that moment brought a
different sort of aloneness. An aloneness
that felt lonely to the bone—a finality.
The pretending was over. I fell to the floor
in heavy tears because I did not have
anyone, but mostly because
I did not have myself.

I had been living in a state of *absolute* disconnection for so long, but in that moment, it felt so visceral. I felt the depth of my own betrayal. I felt the full force of it as a punch to my gut. A betrayal I had let happen over and over again. But I had never fully felt the conscious weight of it until that moment. Until that moment, I had simply been trying to survive.

Where did I go from there? How did I even begin to feel connected to myself again in a pile of rubble?

It took living this question for years to learn that I did not need to go anywhere. It took living this question for years to know that connection could only be found right where I stood.

I needed to learn to stop running. I needed to remember how to listen and how to feel. I needed to face everything I was running from. I needed to remember how to love myself and to realize my worth through that love. I needed to remember that life was worth living—*really living*. I needed to remember that to really live, I needed to really know myself. I had forgotten what that felt like. I needed to give in to fully experiencing everything—that is the only way to know it.

We often attempt to look very far ahead.

We want to know the end before we
begin. We look for shortcuts and ways
around where we are. We need to
let all of that go.

There are no shortcuts

and wouldn't we do ourselves a disservice
in attempting to make them?

Living moment to moment is how we
find the connection to ourselves again.
Moment to moment, layer upon layer,
step by step. Patience becomes
a close friend.

If we stop too abruptly, it can be too
much, and we run the risk
of fleeing again.

It felt so difficult to stand still,
so I learned to slow down.

I began to notice. I began to notice myself
and the things around me. I began to take
time for many things—but *small things*.
The things I learned mean the most.
I began to listen. I began to notice
how I felt when I took time
for such small things.

It seems so simple, yet I had
gone so long without doing so.
It was like I was learning all
over again,

discovering all over again,

the meaning of intimacy.

I let life begin to touch me in
small ways. It is in these small
ways that we slowly begin to
thaw. And as we begin to thaw,
we begin to soften again.
This is love in *motion*.

Can you see how everything, absolutely
everything, is about coming back to love?

Love sees. Love soothes. Love holds. Love
mends. Love strengthens. Love accepts.
Love forgives. Love harmonizes.

Love is the foundation of existence.

We learn to run from it. We run from
ourselves, and we run from others, and
we run from life because we have only
ever been let down by it,

right?

We are never let down by love. We can
only be let down by the absence of it.

Perhaps others say they love,
but that love makes us feel less
than. That is not love.

Perhaps others say they love,
but their actions do not come
from love. When love is spoken
but not embodied, that is not
love.

Perhaps others choose when
they will love—they place
conditions upon giving it. That
is not love.

If this world would only teach
us what love is not, we find
the truth of love living in
between it.

Between our ribs.

                    Between worlds and words.

Between hands.

Between our layers, because
love holds them together.

Through meeting ourselves, we begin to
learn what love is. We get to know it. We
feel its embrace.

Only the presence of love gives us the
strength to face what we wish to forget.

Learning to love means learning to
lose. As we remember love, we must
let go of all that is not an expression of
it—the fears, the masks, the façades,
the relationships, the identities, the
detrimental ways in which we cope.

We may fight to keep such things
because we are afraid of loss. Why are we
so afraid to let go? Who will we be on the
other side? Uncertainty feels like a free
fall. Maybe we do not know how far that
fall is. Maybe it feels like we are losing a
piece of ourselves.

No matter what we might let go of, we
will never lose what is true.

Letting go of things from feeling broken only makes room to experience our wholeness. Through love, we find a resolution from the past. That resolution allows us to feel peace for all of the pieces of ourselves to return home.

We cannot take back time, but we may take our whole selves back from it. This is forgiveness. Forgiveness allows us to see more and more of what is true. In the space beyond time, within the worlds of our hearts, beneath the hardened walls, the jagged exteriors, the buried emotions, and the fears we feel powerless to, our wholeness still lives as the truth.

One of the most profound moments of
my journey was when I began to feel this
wholeness again.

This wholeness began to feel like a
closeness with life around me—so
connected and at peace that it felt like
there was no end to me. I would close
my eyes and feel a part of it all. I was
everywhere all at once.

Perhaps the wings had been there
all along, and now I felt like I could
remember how to fly. It is wholeness that
allows us to experience this freedom. It is
wholeness that allows us to take flight.

This world teaches us that
wholeness comes from
having it all.

Life teaches us that wholeness
comes from being it all.

Perhaps one of the greatest lessons of my life was learning that I was going to disappoint others on the path to the latter. That others were going to misunderstand me, and that what mattered was that I continued to understand myself. That I would continue to do so because who she was was always changing, always evolving.

A lot of my life was spent pleasing others—prioritizing them, being overly agreeable, taking on what was not mine. I had no boundaries. I did not know how to say no. And because I did not know how to say no, I did not know how to say yes. I absolutely did not know how to express my own needs. I did not know what they even were. They were buried beneath the many ways I felt compelled to placate.

I was deeply afraid of being
misunderstood, so I made sure to
perpetually be someone who was
easy to understand.

The thought of disappointing someone
was confronting. The thought of any
fallout was terrifying. I learned to stifle
my needs and my convictions in order to
avoid this disappointment.

Over time—as I chose to honor myself, to
learn my own needs and how to express
them—I inevitably learned the feeling of
being misunderstood. I became the safe
space within myself to be okay with that.

They say the path is narrow. That
is because our path is so wildly and
uniquely our own.

How can we expect every person to
understand a journey we solely are
meant to take? We cannot. There
will inevitably be people who do not
understand it. That is because they are
not meant to walk it.

We will continuously be given the choice to honor this lesson.
It is a choice we must face and a choice we must make, and
when we come out on the other side,

we realize time and time again

that it was never really a choice at all

with the truth as our guiding light.

Because, as we remember,

we will always choose the light that guides us home.

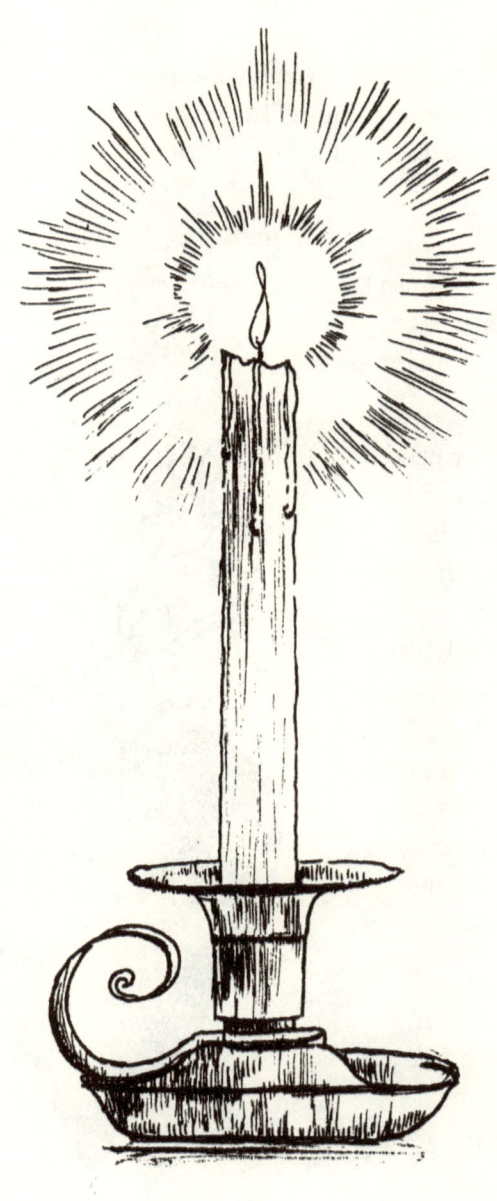

Home is perhaps a feeling we have been searching for our whole lives. This sort of longing lives as an ache that we cannot explain.

To belong. To be seen in truth. To be accepted as that truth.
To be loved unconditionally.

Perhaps we attempted to find that sense of home within another. We hoped that someone else would fill the missing spaces within ourselves. We traveled to different places attempting to fit in, not realizing that if we did not fit within our own skin, it did not matter how far we went.

We will always be led back to ourselves. We are meant to be led back to ourselves.

Life showed me that home is not a place. It is a frequency. It is a feeling. For years and years I searched for this feeling, eventually realizing that to find it is to become it.

Home becomes a place when that frequency is embodied.

What is home meant to feel like?

Home indeed feels like love. It feels like tenderness. It feels like openness. It feels like acceptance. It feels like warmth. It also feels like safety.

This feeling of safety *allows*. It allows us to come home to our bodies. It allows us to be vulnerable. It allows us to be intimate. It allows us to feel and to process. It allows us to express ourselves. It is how we feel alive.

We can only *feel and experience* our way to this space of safety. It is not something we can tell ourselves; it is something we must show ourselves over and over again.

How would you hold something delicate in your hand? With a gentle touch. With reverence, seeing the beauty in every part of it. We can treat ourselves the same way.

There is a tremendous amount that we have faced in this world and we have yet to really face it at all.

Little by little, we learn to hold ourselves
the way we were never held. To come
back to our hearts. To feel compassion
for ourselves, our bodies, and our
experience. To give ourselves space with
unconditional presence. Little by little,
we process what is trapped inside. Little
by little, we learn to let life hold us, too.
We seek support from those we trust
when we need it. We find solace in the
places where we feel safe.

We cannot know
our place within
this living tapestry
when we believe the
very same life is out
to get us.

Because, somewhere along the way, the world tore us apart. We assumed that life would do the same. But for a long time, this world has not been the expression of life. It has been the reversal of it.

Life is complex, but never out to get us.

Perhaps, like me, you never learned the capacity to feel and process the complexities she brings. We lost our faith in her, and we lost faith in ourselves.

It is our choice to embrace an existence where we can hold complexity. It is our choice to find that faith once more in doing so. If we are to experience the possibilities of ourselves and our lives, we must.

Life will challenge us, and she will not
sugarcoat the process. But she will
always stand with us.

She will forever and only call for the
highest expression of ourselves. She
is the expression of love, and love can
only guide us forward. She will bring us
deeper—undoubtedly so—but only so that
we may rise higher. This is our faith; life
wishes for us to thrive in every way.

Sometimes the way forward feels like
we are moving so very backward. As we
meet ourselves, and face things within
ourselves, we have to experience these
things to really see them. Feelings and
emotions will arise. We will sit within
extreme discomfort. The deepest parts
of us wish to be seen, and we can only sit
with them for as long as they need.

Sometimes it will feel like this faith
is all we have.

Sometimes the way forward will cause
us to feel so alone. Everybody talks about
the discomfort in growth. Nobody really
talks about the discomfort that comes
when we grow and we change and others
around us do not.

Again, sometimes it will feel like this
faith is all we have.

This faith shows us that we are
never truly alone.

This faith shows us that the life we truly
wish for, and the life we truly deserve,
is in part already here. Even in times of
discomfort, all we have to do is open our
senses to experience it.

As we open up to ourselves,
and we open ourselves up
to life, we will begin to see
the love and the beauty that
exists all around us because
we have begun to see it within
ourselves. Can we let ourselves
feel it and experience it?

The beauty that exists around us is life
continuously saying, *"I love you."*

This expression of love allows us to find
those same sentiments for ourselves.

Expression is liberation. There are a
great many things that our hearts and
bodies are dying to say. It is a sickening
thing to feel silenced.

Love says, *"I hear you."*

Can you see how we must then give ourselves to life?

When we feel the love that life is expressing, we find more openings within ourselves to say, *"I love me, too."*

Our lives feel so promising when we can genuinely, wholeheartedly, and full-bodily say these words. When these words become a prayer for every breath we take and each step we make.

These words will always wrap around us like the most tender hug.

These words will always soothe, restore, and welcome.

These words will always hold the hope for tomorrow.

Hope for tomorrow is, in part, our
willingness to be with today.
Our willingness to be with what is true
at this moment. Our willingness to be
open to seeing and experiencing this
moment in novel ways.

To be soft. To live in wonder. To ask the questions we are afraid to ask. To live our way to the answers. To tell the truth and let the truth be told to us. To let life continuously show us what we are ready to face and ready to heal. To let her break us open to the truth within our hearts. To recognize our strength as she does.

It is then that life becomes magnificent and meaningful.

This longing we feel so distinctly and
so deeply is the most profound and true
desire to simply know ourselves. To know
ourselves not through the eyes of this
world, but when all of this world has
been stripped away.

To see from the center of it all.

To live from the home within our hearts.

It is the greatest gift to live with this
kind of intimacy. To live with this kind of
vulnerability, honesty, and transparency
and have full authority within it. It is
the safest space to be because it is the
strongest way to stand.

WITHIN ME

When I began this journey—with just
that promise I had made to my heart—I
had no idea that life could feel like this.
The gift that my life would become. That
its beauty could make me weep in
a million ways.

                        That I could only stand in awe of it.

That the complexity of what she is
could, and would, make me weep in
a million more.

                    And that every single moment would be
                    worth it, because it would show me the
                        truth, and it would show me
                            the reason for being.

Within all of that, I would feel the
blessing of breathing again. It would
forge within me the strength and the
reverence needed to carve my own path
because of it all.

At the start, I did not know that my
heart would heal, and that it would
become strong enough, big enough, and
soft enough to hold the whole of the
world. I would be fulfilled and truly alive.
I would sing my song proudly because
it is evidence of who I am and all I have
survived. And I would sing my song for
others, to extend my hand, to show them
they are not alone.

In time, I would be content knowing how deeply woven I was within the music because I could feel it alive within me and around me. This is when peace settles in. This aliveness... it does not take away the complexities of this life—it allows me to *be with them*. It allows me to share my heart with them and to feel the same in return.

I am not quite certain there are words to capture the feeling of what it means to come alive in this way—the peace, the freedom, the possibility, the magic.

I only hope, with every part of me in this world and beyond, that we get to experience it together.

What will it take for you to believe in the peace, the freedom, the possibility, and the magic that lives within your own heart?

What will it take for you to begin living this question, one day at a time?

What will it take to sing the song your soul whispers to you? To *be* that song?

What will it take for you to promise?

Life is waiting with an outstretched
hand for you to come alive and join the
symphony.

ABOUT THE AUTHOR

Kaitlyn Rightmyer is a wandering writer and storyteller. She is also the founder of The Heart Song.

Within Me is her first book. These words are a reflection of her journey and of what is possible no matter what we have endured. She knows the power of vulnerability, and this book is the bearing of her heart. It is her story, but it is also an invitation, and evidence that we can more than survive together.

When she's not creating, you can find her exploring; life is the inspiration for her work. She loves books, coffee, and adventures. All three at the same time are a love story.

Visit www.kaitlynrightmyer.com to learn more about the author, connect with her work, and explore the spaces she's created.